In the series by M. Sasek

THIS IS PARIS (1959)

THIS IS LONDON (1959)

THIS IS ROME (1960)

THIS IS NEW YORK (1960)

THIS IS EDINBURGH (1961)

THIS IS MUNICH (1961)

THIS IS VENICE (1961)

THIS IS SAN FRANCISCO (1962)

THIS IS ISRAEL (1962)

THIS IS CAPE KENNEDY (1963)

THIS IS IRELAND (1964)

THIS IS HONG KONG (1965)

THIS IS GREECE (1966)

THIS IS TEXAS (1967)

THIS IS THE UNITED NATIONS (1968)

THIS IS WASHINGTON, D.C. (1969)

THIS IS AUSTRALIA (1970)

THIS IS HISTORIC BRITAIN (1974)

© Miroslav Sasek, 1974

Printed in Great Britain by Butler & Tanner Ltd, Frome and London

ISBN 0 491 01680 8

M. SASEK

THIS IS HISTORIC BRITAIN

LOCH NESS

BALMORAL
BRAEMAR CASTLE

FORT WILLIAM
△ BEN NEVIS

Scotland

LOCH LOMOND   STIRLING

GLASGOW   EDINBURGH

Northern

BELFAST
Ireland

HADRIAN'S WALL   DURHAM

CARLISLE

YORK

England

CONWAY   CHESTER   LINCOLN

CAERNARVON   LITTLE MORETON HALL

HARLECH

Wales

STRATFORD on AVON   ELY

HEREFORD   CAMBRIDGE   BURY St. EDMUNDS

TEWKESBURY   OXFORD   WOBURN   COLCHESTER

PEMBROKE   MONMOUTH   GLOUCESTER   LONDON

TINTERN ABBEY   WINDSOR

CARDIFF   HAMPTON COURT

BRISTOL   CANTERBURY

BATH

WELLS   STONEHENGE   DOVER

SALISBURY

EXETER   BRIGHTON

W. H. ALLEN

There's such a lot to see, but we've got to start somewhere — so let's start at the Tower of London, by the River Thames. Inside you can see the Crown Jewels, the Beefeaters and the ravens.

6

On the right is Tower Bridge, which divides to let tall ships go through.

When the Royal Standard is flying over Buckingham Palace it means the Queen is in residence. Crowds gather outside the railings each day to watch the Changing of the Guard.

Westminster Abbey is London's most important church. Beyond it you can see the two towers of the Houses of Parliament — on the left, the Clock Tower with Big Ben and on the right, the Victoria Tower . . .

. . . and here are the Houses of Parliament themselves — on the left, the Lords, and on the right, the Commons. This is where the country's laws are passed. You can go inside and watch it happening.

St Paul's Cathedral is in the City of London. Some think it the most beautiful church in London. Just down the road is Fleet Street, where most of Britain's national newspapers are published. Leading off Fleet Street there are many little alleys and courts dating back to the seventeenth century. Many of them are associated with Dr Johnson. He lived in three of them, and in one of them, Wine Office Court, is the Cheshire Cheese, a pub where he and James Boswell used to meet.

The centre of London is the West End — and the very centre is Piccadilly Circus. Most of the big theatres, cinemas and shops are a short walk from here . . .

. . . and so is Trafalgar Square, where Admiral Nelson presides over the lions and pigeons from the top of his column.

A short train — or boat — ride from London, and here we are at Hampton Court, Henry VIII's palace by the Thames. Don't get lost in the maze! Henry used to hunt in the forests around it and you can still see herds of deer in nearby Richmond Park. Less wild are the botanical gardens of Kew, just down the river.

Woburn Abbey is the home of the Duke of Bedford. As you can see it's very handsome. It also has a wildlife park and a zoo. Queen Elizabeth I visited the Abbey in 1572, but the Earl of Bedford hoped she would stay no more than a day and two nights.

And this is Windsor Castle, another royal palace, set in a pretty country town. The view from the Round Tower is said to include twelve counties. English kings and queens have lived in the castle since the eleventh century. Here is Castle Hill . . .

. . . and here is another view of Windsor Castle, this time from the Thames. On the opposite side of the river from the castle is Eton village with its famous school, founded in 1440. Further down the river, a short distance from Windsor, are the Runny-mede meadows, where, on the 12th of June 1215, King John reluctantly signed the Magna Carta. The Kennedy Memorial is in the same field.

This little crooked house in Windsor is called Market Cross House. It was bought in 1656 for £82 by one William Bradbury. Beside it is the Guildhall, built by Sir Christopher Wren, who designed St Paul's Cathedral.

Oxford is the second oldest university in Europe. This college, Christ Church, was founded in 1525 by Cardinal Wolsey. We are in its main square, Tom Quad (short for 'quadrangle'), facing Tom Tower.

Corpus Christi College is older — it was started in 1516. It is one of the smaller colleges. We can't see any of the under-graduates (the students) in their black gowns; they must be on vacation.

Mob Quad, in Merton College, dates back to the Middle Ages, as far as 1264, in fact. The university at Oxford was probably first started by some students who had been expelled from Paris University.

The Bodleian Library is one of the oldest in the world. It is full of many very rare manuscripts and books.

No tour of Britain would be complete without a visit to Shakespeare's town of Stratford-upon-Avon. This is the house where he was born. It is still perfectly preserved . . .

. . . and so is New Place, which is not new at all, and where he died. There are lots of other lovely Tudor houses in Stratford such as Hall's croft where John Hall, Shakespeare's son-in-law, lived. Stratford is much older than Shakespeare's time though; people have lived there since the Bronze Age.

The church of Holy Trinity, where Shakespeare was buried . . .

. . . and his memorial, inside the church.

Here is the home of John Harvard's mother — he was the founder of America's Harvard University.

This is Chester Cathedral. Chester is a very old town. In 'The Rows' the medieval houses have an overhanging first floor, converting the narrow road into a shady corridor. Not far away, in the village of Neston, the future Lady Hamilton grew up in poverty, later to become Horatio Nelson's mistress and one of the most famous women of her time.

From this tower Charles I watched the progress of his troops in the battle of Rowton Moor. It has since been named King Charles' Tower.

There are quite a few black and white 'herring-bone' half-timbered houses like this in Cheshire. This one is Little Moreton Hall. Not far away is Knutsford, the town Mrs Gaskell described as 'Cranford'. We are still in Cheshire, but only a little way north is the River Mersey and Liverpool, in Lancashire, where the Beatles came from.

Carlisle Castle is one of a series of medieval fortresses on the border built to defend the English against the Scots. It did not fall until 1745, when Bonnie Prince Charlie rode into Carlisle on a white horse, with a hundred pipers marching in front of him. But before long he was on his way home to Scotland, after being beaten by the English at Derby.

Hadrian's Wall was built by the Romans, also to keep the Scots out of Britain. Originally it ran from Carlisle in the west to Newcastle in the east, and much of it is still standing.

The whole town of Durham was once confined to a bend in the River Weir which doubles back on itself, nearly making a small island. You can see the old town, with the Cathedral and castle on the other side of the bridge in the picture. Now much of the old town has been taken over by the university, and the great hall of the castle is the students' dining room.

Yorkshire, the largest county in England, is famous for its moors, its pudding and the city of York, whose principal church is called The Minster. Here it is. It has a very famous stained-glass window called the Five Sisters. The whole building took two and a half centuries to complete. Not far away, near the River Ouse, is the site of one of the major battles of the Civil War — Marston Moor.

York is one of many British cities whose ancient outer walls have survived. In the York Museum you can see life-size reconstructions of old York streets, complete with shops, vehicles and people. You can also drive out onto the famous Yorkshire moors to the Brontë country, and visit their old home in Haworth, near Keighley — now a museum.

Lincoln Cathedral contains one of the original copies of the Magna Carta. In the town there is a castle founded by William the Conqueror, and a gateway that has been in use since Roman times. Not very far away is Somersby, where Tennyson was born, and Grantham where Isaac Newton went to school. Near Lincoln is the town of Boston, after which Boston in Massachusetts was named.

Ely Cathedral is one of the major monuments of East Anglia. You can see it for miles around because the countryside is so flat. It is in the Isle of Ely, which isn't an island at all, but a part of Cambridgeshire.

The house in Ely where Oliver Cromwell, leader of the Roundheads in the English Civil War, lived from 1636 to 1647. Cromwell also had a farm in the village of Stuntney, a mile south-east of Ely. From this village you will find the very best view of the Cathedral.

It would never do to mention Oxford and not Cambridge. After all, in the annual boat-race between the two universities, Cambridge has won more times. This is Trinity College, and we are in the Great Court.

The President's Lodge at Queen's College. There are about 7,200 undergraduates in residence at Cambridge, some 800 fewer than at Oxford.

This is another college, the oldest in Cambridge. It's simply called Peterhouse.

Here is King's College. The white building in the middle is the College Chapel, which has a very famous choir.

Bury St Edmunds is a beautiful Georgian town in Suffolk. This well-preserved gateway leads to the fourteenth-century abbey. You can just see the portcullis that they used to lower to keep out attackers. It's a long time since anybody attacked the abbey, though.

The abbey itself is more of a romantic ruin. In the nearby Stour Valley Constable painted many landscapes.

Not far from Bury is Colchester, the oldest recorded town in England. This is what's left of its Norman Castle. There used to be water in the moat, but now you can stroll around in it. It was near here that Queen Boadicea led her army in revolt against the Romans.

At this spot Thomas Becket, the Archbishop of Canterbury, was murdered in 1170, by four knights who mistakenly thought King Henry II wanted to get rid of him. Afterwards the king was very sorry, and the cathedral became a centre for pilgrims from all over Europe. Chaucer's *Canterbury Tales* is about a group of these pilgrims, telling each other stories on their way to St Thomas' shrine.

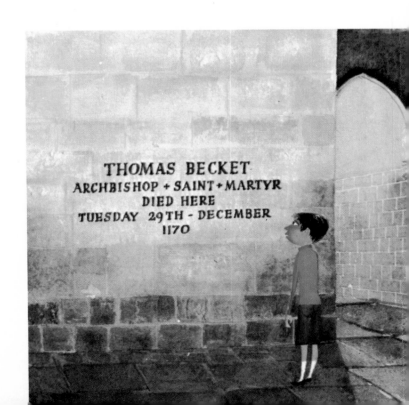

THOMAS BECKET
ARCHBISHOP + SAINT + MARTYR
DIED HERE
TUESDAY 29TH - DECEMBER
1170

Opposite is Canterbury Cathedral. Canterbury is the county town of Kent. All over the county you will see field after field of hops, used for making beer, and the oast-houses in which the hops are dried. This is one of the reasons why Kent is known as the Garden of England. In the western part of the county is Chartwell, Sir Winston Churchill's beautiful Tudor home, now a museum.

The West Gate of Canterbury has hardly altered in the last six hundred years. One addition is a museum inside it.

There is also an abbey at Canterbury. It was founded by St Augustine, and is outside the city walls. Until the death of St Thomas Becket it was more important than the cathedral.

Brighton in Sussex is the best known of the many English seaside resorts. It has miles of beaches and a dolphinarium, a sort of circus with dolphins, and lovely Regency buildings. Until 1724 Brighton was just a small fishing town. Then sea-bathing became fashionable, and the Prince Regent built this extraordinary palace, the Royal Pavilion, and took his court to Brighton.

Dover is the nearest English town to France. On a clear day you can see the French coast from these cliffs — the famous White Cliffs of Dover. Dover used to be the chief of the 'Cinque Ports'. There is a Norman castle overlooking the sea, and the remains of a Roman lighthouse inside its grounds.

Salisbury has the tallest cathedral in Britain. It was built in the thirteenth century, and the spire is 404 feet high. Unfortunately the foundations were not strong enough to take so great a weight and in the library there is a report from the eighteenth-century architect, Sir Christopher Wren, on the condition of the spire.

Salisbury Plain also contains another remarkable monument — the circle of gigantic stones known as Stonehenge. It was built more than three thousand years ago. Nobody quite knows why it was built; perhaps as a huge astronomical instrument to calculate the movement of the sun, or perhaps as a place for sun worship. Despite their enormous size the stones were brought all the way from Wales and are very accurately placed. Stonehenge, and the nearby Avebury Ring, are full of mysteries. Bronze Age axes which have been found on the site are similar to some discovered at prehistoric Mycenae in Greece. How did they get there?

And now we're in the West Country. Devon is famous for its cream and its sailors. The Pilgrim Fathers sailed to America from Plymouth in the *Mayflower*, and on the Hoe in Plymouth Sir Francis Drake played bowls while the Spanish Armada approached. Exeter is the capital of Devon. It is a very old town, first founded by the Romans. The picture shows Exeter Cathedral; two of its towers were built in 1050, but the rest is a little more modern. In the Cathedral Close there is a shop which used to be Mol's Coffee House, where it is said that Drake, Hawkins and others used to meet.

And this is the Guildhall, built in the fifteenth century. Underneath Exeter are medieval passages built over streams which used to provide the town with a constant supply of fresh spring water.

Wells Cathedral, in Somerset, the 'cider country'. Inside
the cathedral there is a remarkable fourteenth-century
clock, across whose face knights joust on the striking
of the hours. Nearby is the thirteenth-century bishop's
palace, where the swans in the moat ring a bell near
the drawbridge when they are hungry. Wells shares its
bishop with Bath . . .

... which is named after these Roman baths, built over a natural spring of hot water. People have been coming here for nearly a thousand years to cure their ailments in the waters. The Roman town was called Aquae Sulis, but another town grew up in its place and the Roman baths weren't re-discovered until the nineteenth century. Eighteenth-century Bath grew into a spa — a fashionable society resort — and many streets of beautiful houses were built, some in a perfect curve, like the Royal Crescent. Behind the baths in the picture you can see the abbey.

Bristol has a long history as a seaport, and many explorers and merchants started their voyages from there. Among them was John Cabot, who sailed from Bristol in 1497 and discovered the mainland of America. For his discovery he was paid the princely sum of £12 and a £20-a-year pension by Henry VII. The hundred-foot Cabot Tower in the picture was named after him.

Many of Bristol's medieval and renaissance buildings were destroyed during the last war. Among the survivors is this inn, the Llandoger Trow ('trow' means 'barge'), built in 1664. It is said that Daniel Defoe first heard here the story he turned into *Robinson Crusoe*, and also that Robert Louis Stevenson used it as the setting for part of *Treasure Island*. In the same street you can see the famous Theatre Royal which was built in 1764 and is probably the oldest playhouse still in use in this country.

The old town of Gloucester began as a Roman fort. Many of the streets still follow the old Roman roads. It was in Gloucester that William the Conqueror decided to make the survey of England known as the *Domesday Book*. This is the eleventh-century cathedral with its 225-foot pinnacled tower. It took nearly a hundred years to build. Inside is the medieval Great Peter Bell, which weighs three tons.

This is Tewkesbury Cathedral. Near here one of the bloodiest battles in the Wars of the Roses was fought, and the site is still known as 'Bloody Meadow'. Tewkesbury has a great many old houses and half-timbered inns. Among them is the 'Hop Pole', before whose 14th-century fireplace Dickens' character Mr Pickwick warmed himself, and ate such a large meal that he slept for the next thirty miles of his journey.

Another of the sights of Tewkesbury is this fine old mill. From its windows you can look across at the outer walls of the abbey buildings, and the monks' granary.

There has been a church on the site of Hereford Cathedral since 825. In Hereford's market place in 1802, a man auctioned off his wife for £1 4s and a bowl of punch!

Mappa Mundi is Latin for 'map of the world'. This one, in Hereford Cathedral, shows the world as it was thought to be in the 13th century — flat. Much of the world, including America, had not been charted then.

King Stephen was supposed to have sat in this chair. He reigned over England — rather in-efficiently — early in the twelfth century.

This is Wales! There are lots of castles in this small country. This one is at Cardiff. It is Norman, but it's hidden behind a facade designed by a Victorian architect, William Burges, when it was the home of the Marquess of Bute. Cardiff itself is an old seaport, and through the ages it has always been full of sailors, including parties of pirates who used to come ashore and frighten the townsfolk. Now Cardiff is the quiet principal city of Wales, and there are no more pirates.

But there is a Welsh Folk Museum at nearby St Fagan's. Here are assembled objects recalling Welsh life in the past, even including complete buildings brought here in pieces and reassembled at the museum.

46

Tintern Abbey, on the River Wye, was founded in 1131, but was dissolved by Henry VIII, and only some of the buildings still stand. Looking down on the abbey from the hills, the poet Wordsworth was so impressed by the beauty of the scene that he wrote a poem about it.

Monmouth is a border town and it has always been disputed whether it belongs to England or Wales. The Monnow Bridge has a fortified gatehouse, built in 1272. It was used for collecting the tolls — three pence for every ship laden with goods for sale in Monmouth, and four pence for every bag of wool.

Monmouth is especially famous for two people: King Henry V, victor of the Battle of Agincourt, and the Hon. Charles Stewart Rolls, co-founder of the Rolls-Royce motor car company and the first man to fly the English Channel both ways. Both are commemorated by statues in front of the eighteenth-century Shire Hall. Henry V is in a niche on the wall below the clock, and Rolls has a pedestal in the square.

This is Conway Castle, known in Welsh as Aberconwy. The old town is still contained within its medieval walls and the castle still stands much as it did in 1295, when King Edward I, who built the castle, was besieged by the Welsh under Llywelyn, the last of the independent Welsh princes.

Conway claims to have the oldest house in Wales, and also the smallest house in Britain — this nineteenth-century fisherman's cottage on the quay. It is 72 inches wide and 122 inches high, and has two tiny rooms and a staircase.

49

Caernarvon is where the investiture of the Prince of Wales is held, because it was in this castle that Edward I presented his own new-born son to the Welsh after he had killed their Prince Llywelyn in battle. Prince Charles was made Prince of Wales here by the Queen in 1969. This is Castle Square .

. . . and this is what the castle looks like from the other side. It was built by Edward I to help keep his hold on Wales. The area enclosed by the castle walls is three acres and the walls themselves are seven to nine feet thick. A short drive from Caernarvon is Portmeirion, a village created by the architect Clough William-Ellis to show that new building doesn't have to disfigure the countryside. His gaily-coloured, unusually-shaped houses nestle prettily on the edge of hills and behind trees.

Harlech Castle is yet another of Edward I's Welsh castles. It was completed in 1283. In the Wars of the Roses it was the last stronghold of the Lancastrians. Margaret of Anjou fled there after their defeat by the Yorkists.

Pembroke Castle, just outside the port of Milford Haven. It is surrounded on three sides by the tides of the Haven (or harbour). Henry Tudor grew up in the castle before he was exiled to Brittany. In 1485 he returned there before the Battle of Bosworth in which he defeated Richard III and gained the crown of England, as Henry VII.

And this is Scotland! Edinburgh Castle, surrounded by the rambling streets of the old town, sits high above the new town and the surrounding lowland, on a large piece of volcanic rock. Perched at the very top is St Margaret's Chapel, which is only large enough to hold twenty-six people. The kings and queens of Scotland have always lived in the castle. It was here, in a tiny room, that Mary Queen of Scots gave birth to James I.

From outside the Castle, the Royal Mile leads down a fascinating street, full of ancient houses, dark courtyards and narrow, curving stone stairways, to the royal palace of Holyroodhouse. It was not until the reign of James IV that the official palace was built, next to a very old abbey, and in 1543 it was partly burned down during an English invasion. Mary Queen of Scots lived in the remaining part of the house, and here, in a room you can still visit, her secretary Rizzio was murdered.

Linlithgow Palace in West Lothian is one of
Scotland's four Royal Palaces. James V and
Mary Queen of Scots were born here.

Here is Braemar Castle, built on a knoll above the River
Dee. It was started in 1628 but has been much altered
since then. Every September at Braemar are held the
Highland Games, known as 'the gathering'. It is famous
all over the world and the Queen always attends.

Balmoral Castle in Aberdeenshire, the personal holiday
home of the Queen. It was built for Queen Victoria and
she spent much of her time here. She called it 'this dear
paradise'. One of her favourite views was at Killiecrankie
on Loch Tommel, now known as 'the Queen's View'.

Stirling Castle is in a very important position on the road to the Highlands, and during any wars always became a centre of fighting. The famous battle of Bannockburn in 1314 was fought over it. There was much fighting between the English and the Scots before they were united. In Inverness you can visit the site of the Battle of Culloden, where the English and the Campbells cruelly slaughtered the retreating Scots.

Fort William is not a fort but a town. It is on the east shore of Loch Linnhe, with Ben Nevis towering behind. There used to be a fort here but it was demolished in the last century to make way for a railway. Ben Nevis is 4,418 feet high and is the highest mountain in the British Isles.

Scotland is full of beautiful long lochs. This is Loch Lomond. It is twenty-four miles long and the largest stretch of inland water in Great Britain. Many think it is also the most beautiful. There are a number of islands in the loch. One contains the ruins of an old castle, another is the burial-place of the clan MacGregor. Another loch in Scotland, Loch Ness, is supposed to contain an enormous monster. Many people say they have seen it, some even have a photograph of it, but no one can prove it exists.